tapas mezze antipasto
& other bites

THE AUSTRALIAN
Women's Weekly

contents

An enticing selection of small Mediterranean dishes served simultaneously is a very appealing way to dine, and the recipes inside are meant to inspire many a long, lingering meal with friends and family alike. Whether served with a glass of wine on a sunny afternoon round a table in the yard or with drinks before dinner, tapas, antipasto and mezze bites never disappoint: mouth-wateringly delicious; unpretentious, "real" foods that excite the palate with their simple yet enormous variety of tastes and textures.

Pamela Clark

Food Director

That Mediterranean smorgasbord of little bites variously called tapas, antipasto and mezze all hail from the region bordering the sea's shores. From Spain to Italy through Greece, Turkey and around the Levant, these titbits are as indicative of a way of life as they are examples of local cuisine. For the people living in this part of the world, eating is a social occasion, more often than not consumed out of doors thanks to days filled with lingering sunshine and a hot, dry climate for much of the year. Sitting in a street-side cafe or under a grape arbour with a coffee or a drink, chatting over a day's events, wouldn't be the same without small plates of flavourful foods that are consumed leisurely but with consummate enthusiasm. Tapas, antipasto and mezze also serve to stave off late-afternoon hunger pangs in countries where the siesta and late working hours mean that the evening meal might not be taken until 9 or 10 at night. This long culinary tradition of Southern Europe is now a fixture among the countries of Northern Europe and North America, too, thanks to travel experiences and migration patterns. Sitting, enjoying the conversation, drink in hand at a long table filled with plates of simple, delicious food, tasting a bit of this and a bite of that – who among us doesn't enjoy it? Here, our selection is easily reproduced at home and perfect for parties, providing a variety of combinations for a balance of exciting tastes and complementary textures: all little plates but so big on flavour that you'll find your guests lingering for hours.

TASTES OF THE MEDITERRANEAN

butter bean dip with pitta crisps

preparation time 10 minutes cooking time 8 minutes makes 1 cup

1 clove garlic, crushed

¼ cup lightly packed fresh flat-leaf parsley leaves

400g can butter beans, rinsed, drained

1 teaspoon ground cumin

⅓ cup (80ml) olive oil

6 pocket pitta, cut into sixths

1 Preheat oven to 200°C/180°C fan-forced.
2 Blend or process garlic, parsley, beans and cumin until combined. With motor operating, add the oil in a thin stream until mixture is smooth.
3 Place pitta pieces on lightly greased oven trays; bake about 8 minutes or until browned lightly.
4 Serve dip with pitta crisps.
   per tablespoon 5.5g fat; 493kJ (118 cal)

DIPS

trio of dips

These three dips will keep in the refrigerator for up to three days; store covered with a thin layer of olive oil. Serve with an assortment of fresh vegetables and grissini (bread sticks).

pistou (basil dip)

preparation time 5 minutes **makes** 1 cup

100g fresh basil leaves

⅔ cup (160ml) olive oil

1 clove garlic, quartered

2 teaspoons finely grated lemon rind

2 tablespoons finely grated parmesan

1 Blend or process ingredients until smooth.
per tablespoon 12.6g fat; 481kJ (115 cal)

tapenade (olive dip)

preparation time 5 minutes **makes** 1½ cups

2½ cups (300g) seeded black olives

2 tablespoons drained capers, rinsed

1 clove garlic, quartered

2 tablespoons lemon juice

1 tablespoon fresh flat-leaf parsley leaves

⅓ cup (80ml) olive oil

1 Blend or process ingredients until smooth.
per tablespoon 4.2g fat; 230kJ (55 cal)

anchoiade (anchovy dip)

preparation time 5 minutes **makes** 1 cup

40 drained anchovy fillets

1 tablespoon lemon juice

2 cloves garlic, quartered

3 teaspoons fresh lemon thyme leaves

⅓ cup (80ml) olive oil

2 tablespoons hot water

1 Blend or process anchovies, juice, garlic and thyme until smooth. With motor operating, add oil in a thin, steady stream until mixture thickens. Transfer to bowl; stir in the water.
per tablespoon 7.3g fat; 330kJ (79 cal)

baba ghanoush

preparation time 15 minutes cooking time 30 minutes (plus standing time) makes 2 cups

2 large eggplants (1kg)
3 cloves garlic, crushed
2 tablespoons tahini
¼ cup (60ml) lemon juice
2 tablespoons olive oil
½ teaspoon sweet paprika

1   Preheat grill.
2   Pierce eggplants all over with fork or skewer; place on oiled oven tray. Grill about 30 minutes or until skin blackens and eggplant is soft, turning occasionally. Stand 15 minutes.
3   Peel eggplants, discard skin; drain eggplants in colander 10 minutes then blend or process with remaining ingredients.
    per tablespoon 8g fat; 431kJ (103 cal)

guacamole

preparation time 10 minutes makes 2½ cups

3 medium avocados (750g)
½ small red onion (50g), chopped finely
1 small egg tomato (60g), seeded, chopped finely
1 tablespoon lime juice
¼ cup coarsely chopped fresh coriander

1   Mash avocados in medium bowl; stir in remaining ingredients.
    per tablespoon 4g fat; 159kJ (38 cal)

turkish spinach dip

preparation time 10 minutes cooking time 10 minutes (plus cooling and refrigeration time) makes 2 cups

1 tablespoon olive oil

1 small brown onion (80g), chopped finely

1 clove garlic, crushed

1 teaspoon ground cumin

½ teaspoon curry powder

¼ teaspoon ground turmeric

100g trimmed spinach leaves, shredded finely

500g thick yogurt

1 Heat oil in medium frying pan; cook onion and garlic, stirring, until onion softens. Add spices; cook, stirring, until fragrant. Add spinach; cook, stirring, until spinach wilts. Transfer mixture to serving bowl; cool.

2 Stir yogurt through mixture, cover; refrigerate 1 hour.

3 Serve cold with toasted pitta, if desired.
per tablespoon 1.5g fat; 100kJ (24 cal)

sweet chilli cream cheese

preparation time 5 minutes makes 2 cups

250g cream cheese, softened
½ cup (120g) sour cream
½ cup (125ml) sweet chilli sauce
¼ cup coarsely chopped fresh coriander

1 Beat cream cheese, sour cream and sauce in small bowl with electric mixer until smooth; stir in coriander.
2 Serve with strips of capsicum, if desired.
   per tablespoon 5.6g fat; 251kJ (60 cal)

hummus

preparation 10 minutes makes 2¼ cups

2 x 300g cans chickpeas, rinsed, drained
2 tablespoons tahini
⅓ cup (80ml) lemon juice
3 cloves garlic, quartered
¼ cup (60ml) water
½ cup (125ml) olive oil

1 Blend or process chickpeas, tahini, juice, garlic and the water until almost smooth. With motor operating, gradually add oil in a thin, steady stream until mixture forms a smooth paste.
2 Serve with carrot sticks, if desired.
   per tablespoon 5.4g fat; 268kJ (64 cal)

blue cheese and caramelised onion dip

preparation time 20 minutes **cooking time** 15 minutes (plus cooing time) **makes** 2 cups

1 tablespoon olive oil

1 medium brown onion (150g), chopped finely

1 medium pear (230g), chopped coarsely

½ cup (150g) mayonnaise

½ cup (125ml) cream

150g danish blue cheese

1 Heat oil in medium frying pan; cook onion, stirring constantly, about 10 minutes or until onion is browned and slightly caramelised. Add pear; cook 5 minutes. Cool.

2 Blend or process mayonnaise, cream and cheese until smooth; transfer to serving bowl. Stir in onion mixture.

3 Serve at room temperature with toasted rye bread fingers, if desired.
per tablespoon 7.1g fat; 334kJ (80 cal)

crab dip

preparation time 10 minutes **makes** 2 cups

200g cream cheese

¼ cup (75g) mayonnaise

2 tablespoons lime juice

1 tablespoon sweet chilli sauce

1 dill pickle, chopped finely

2 x 170g cans crab meat, drained, flaked

2 tablespoons finely chopped fresh coriander

1 Beat cream cheese, mayonnaise, juice and sauce in small bowl with electric mixer until smooth. Transfer to serving bowl; fold in remaining ingredients.

2 Serve cold with toasted french bread slices, if desired.
per tablespoon 3.8g fat; 205kJ (49 cal)

17

ricotta and green olive dip

preparation time 5 minutes makes 1 cup

½ cup (100g) low-fat ricotta

¼ cup (40g) finely chopped seeded green olives

1 crushed clove garlic

¼ cup finely chopped fresh chives

¼ cup finely chopped fresh flat-leaf parsley

1 teaspoon finely grated lemon rind

1 tablespoon lemon juice

1 Combine ingredients in small bowl.

2 Serve with baby carrots, if desired.

per tablespoon 1g fat; 75kJ (18 cal)

beetroot dip

preparation time 5 minutes makes 2½ cups

850g can beetroot slices, drained

1 clove garlic, quartered

¼ cup (60g) sour cream

1 tablespoon tahini

1 tablespoon lemon juice

1 Blend or process ingredients until smooth.

2 Serve with whole wheat crackers, if desired.

per tablespoon 1.2g fat; 88kJ (21 cal)

risotto-filled zucchini flowers

preparation time 50 minutes cooking time 50 minutes makes 48

1 cup (250ml) dry white wine

2 cups (500ml) vegetable stock

½ cup (125ml) water

1 tablespoon olive oil

1 small brown onion (80g), chopped finely

1 clove garlic, crushed

1 cup (200g) arborio rice

150g mushrooms, sliced thinly

2 trimmed silver beet leaves (160g), chopped finely

¼ cup (20g) finely grated parmesan

48 tiny zucchini with flowers attached

1 Combine wine, stock and the water in large saucepan; bring to a boil, simmer, covered.

2 Meanwhile, heat oil in large saucepan; cook onion and garlic, stirring, until onion softens. Add rice; stir to coat in onion mixture. Stir in 1 cup of the hot stock mixture; cook, stirring, over low heat until liquid is absorbed. Continue adding hot stock mixture, in 1-cup batches, stirring, until liquid is absorbed after each addition. Total cooking time should be about 35 minutes or until rice is tender.

3 Add mushrooms and silver beet; cook, stirring, until mushrooms are just tender. Stir in cheese.

4 Remove and discard stamens from centre of flowers; fill flowers with risotto, twist petal tops to enclose filling.

5 Cook zucchini with flowers, in batches, on heated oiled grill plate (or grill or barbecue) until zucchini are just tender and risotto is heated through.
per flower 0.7g fat; 121kJ (29 cal)

VEGETABLES

asparagus with three toppings

preparation time 15 minutes cooking time 15 minutes serves 6

asparagus with anchovies and garlic

200g asparagus, trimmed

2 tablespoons extra virgin olive oil

1 clove garlic, sliced thinly

3 anchovies, drained, chopped coarsely

freshly ground black pepper

1　Preheat oven to 200°C/180°C fan-forced.

2　Place asparagus in shallow baking dish; pour over the combined oil, garlic, anchovies and pepper. Toss asparagus to coat in oil mixture.

3　Roast about 5 minutes or until asparagus is just tender.

per serving 6.3g fat; 272kJ (65 cal)

asparagus with butter and parmesan

200g asparagus, trimmed

20g unsalted butter, melted

2 tablespoons parmesan flakes

½ teaspoon freshly ground black pepper

1　Boil, steam or microwave asparagus until just tender.

2　Serve drizzled with melted butter and sprinkled with parmesan and pepper.

per serving 3.5g fat; 171kJ (41 cal)

asparagus with balsamic dressing

200g asparagus, trimmed

1 large tomato (220g), chopped finely

2 tablespoons extra virgin olive oil

3 teaspoons balsamic vinegar

½ teaspoon freshly ground black pepper

1 tablespoon small basil leaves

1　Cook asparagus on heated, lightly oiled grill plate (or grill or barbecue) about 5 minutes or until tender.

2　Serve sprinkled with combined tomato, oil, vinegar and pepper; top with basil.

per serving 6.1g fat; 280kJ (67 cal)

mini zucchini frittatas

preparation time 20 minutes cooking time 15 minutes makes 24

4 eggs

½ cup (120g) sour cream

2 tablespoons finely chopped fresh chives

1 small yellow zucchini (90g), grated coarsely

1 small green zucchini (90g), grated coarsely

2 tablespoons finely grated parmesan

1 tablespoon coarsely chopped fresh chives, extra

1 Preheat oven to 180°C/160°C fan-forced. Lightly oil two 12-hole mini (1½ tablespoons/30ml) muffin pans.

2 Whisk eggs with two-thirds of the sour cream in large bowl until smooth; stir in chives, zucchini and cheese.

3 Divide mixture among pan holes. Bake, uncovered, 15 minutes; turn onto wire rack to cool. Top frittatas with remaining sour cream and extra chives.
per frittata 3.1g fat; 142kJ (34 cal)

artichoke hearts in white-wine vinaigrette

preparation time 45 minutes cooking time 30 minutes (plus cooling time) serves 4

1 medium lemon (140g), chopped coarsely

20 small globe artichokes (2kg)

2 cups (500ml) dry white wine

¼ cup loosely packed fresh thyme leaves

5 cloves garlic, unpeeled

½ cup (125ml) lemon juice

2 teaspoons sea salt flakes

1 cup (250ml) white wine vinegar

2 cups (500ml) water

1 tablespoon extra virgin olive oil

1 Cut a piece of baking paper into a circle to fit inside large saucepan.

2 Place lemon in large bowl half-filled with cold water.

3 Discard outer leaves from artichokes; cut tips from remaining leaves. Trim then peel stalks; place artichokes in lemon water.

4 Combine wine, thyme, garlic, juice, salt, vinegar, the water and drained artichokes in large saucepan; cover with baking-paper round; bring to a boil. Simmer, covered, about 25 minutes or until artichokes are just tender. Cool in poaching liquid 30 minutes. Whisk ½ cup (125ml) of the poaching liquid in small bowl with oil (discard remaining liquid).

5 Halve artichokes vertically; using small knife, remove chokes. Divide artichokes among serving bowls; drizzle with poaching liquid mixture.
per serving 5.5g fat; 912kJ (218 cal)

pea pakoras with coriander raita

preparation time 25 minutes cooking time 15 minutes makes 24

1½ cups (225g) besan flour

½ teaspoon bicarbonate of soda

¾ cup (180ml) water

2 teaspoons vegetable oil

2 cloves garlic, crushed

½ teaspoon ground turmeric

½ teaspoon cumin seeds

1 teaspoon ground cumin

½ teaspoon dried chilli flakes

1 tablespoon coarsely chopped fresh coriander

1 cup (120g) frozen peas

2 green onions, chopped finely

40g baby spinach leaves, shredded coarsely

vegetable oil, for deep-frying, extra

CORIANDER RAITA

1 cup (280g) Greek-style yogurt

1 cup firmly packed coarsely chopped coriander

½ teaspoon ground cumin

1 Sift flour and soda into medium bowl; whisk in the water to form a smooth batter.

2 Heat oil in small saucepan; cook garlic and spices, stirring, until fragrant. Add to the batter mixture with coriander, peas, onion and spinach; mix well.

3 Heat extra oil in wok; deep-fry level tablespoons of the mixture, in batches, about 5 minutes or until browned lightly. Drain on absorbent paper.

4 Make coriander raita.

5 Serve pakoras with coriander raita.

   CORIANDER RAITA Blend or process ingredients until smooth.
   per serving 3.9g fat; 305kJ (73 cal)

potato and goat's cheese fritters

preparation time 10 minutes cooking time 20 minutes makes 32

600g potatoes, chopped coarsely

¼ cup (60ml) cream

¼ teaspoon ground nutmeg

3 eggs, beaten lightly

2 egg yolks, beaten lightly

½ cup (75g) plain flour

250g firm goat cheese, crumbled

2 tablespoons coarsely chopped
fresh flat-leaf parsley

pinch cayenne pepper

vegetable oil, for deep-frying

1 Boil, steam or microwave potatoes until tender; drain. Mash potatoes in large bowl with cream and nutmeg until smooth. Add eggs and egg yolks; using a wooden spoon, beat until smooth. Stir in flour, cheese, parsley and pepper.

2 Heat oil in large saucepan; deep-fry level tablespoons of the potato mixture, in batches, until fritters are browned lightly. Drain on absorbent paper.
per fritter 4.8g fat; 288kJ (69 cal)

garlic mushrooms

preparation time 10 minutes cooking time 10 minutes serves 8

90g butter, chopped

3 cloves garlic, crushed

750g button mushrooms, halved if large

1 tablespoon lemon juice

2 tablespoons coarsely chopped fresh
flat-leaf parsley

1 teaspoon sea salt

½ teaspoon freshly ground black pepper

1 Melt butter in medium saucepan; cook garlic, stirring, until fragrant.

2 Add mushrooms; stir to coat in butter mixture. Cook, covered, over high heat, stirring occasionally, until mushrooms are almost tender.

3 Remove lid; bring to a boil. Boil until liquid is reduced by half and mushrooms are tender.

4 Stir in remaining ingredients.
per serving 9.6g fat; 464kJ (111 cal)

vegetable fritters with tzatziki

preparation time 20 minutes (plus refrigeration time) **cooking** 20 minutes **serves** 8

4 medium zucchini (480g), grated coarsely

1 teaspoon salt

1 medium brown onion (150g), chopped finely

¾ cup (50g) stale breadcrumbs

2 eggs, beaten lightly

1 tablespoon finely chopped fresh oregano

1 tablespoon finely chopped fresh mint

2 tablespoons extra virgin olive oil

TZATZIKI

2 cups (560g) thick Greek-style yogurt

1 lebanese cucumber (130g)

1 clove garlic, crushed

2 tablespoons finely chopped fresh mint

2 tablespoons lemon juice

½ teaspoon sea salt

1   Make tzatziki.

2   Combine zucchini and salt in medium bowl; stand 15 minutes then squeeze out excess liquid. Combine zucchini with onion, breadcrumbs, egg, oregano and mint in medium bowl.

3   Heat oil in large frying pan; cook tablespoonfuls of zucchini mixture, flattened slightly, in batches, until browned on both sides and cooked through. Drain on absorbent paper; cover to keep warm.

4   Serve fritters with tzatziki.

TZATZIKI Line sieve with absorbent paper, place over bowl; place yogurt in sieve. Cover, refrigerate at least 4 hours; discard liquid from bowl. Halve cucumber lengthways; remove seeds. Coarsely grate flesh and skin. Squeeze out excess liquid. Combine yogurt, cucumber, garlic, mint, juice and salt in bowl.

per serving 11.2g fat; 786kJ (188 cal)

cajun potato wedges

preparation time 10 minutes cooking time 40 minutes serves 4

1kg kipfler potatoes, unpeeled

2 tablespoons olive oil

½ teaspoon ground oregano

2 teaspoons ground cumin

1 teaspoon hot paprika

½ teaspoon ground black pepper

1 teaspoon ground turmeric

1 teaspoon ground coriander

¼ teaspoon chilli powder

1 Preheat oven to 200°C/180°C fan-forced. Lightly oil two oven trays.
2 Cut each potato into wedges; toss potato with remaining ingredients in large bowl.
3 Place wedges, in single layer, on trays; roast, uncovered, turning occasionally, about 40 minutes or until crisp and cooked through.
per serving 10.3g fat; 1082kJ (259 cal)

mushrooms with fetta on garlic croûtes

preparation time 10 minutes cooking time 10 minutes serves 4

500g swiss brown mushrooms

½ cup (125ml) extra virgin olive oil

12 cherry tomatoes, halved

8 slices crusty italian bread

1 clove garlic, halved

2 tablespoons shredded fresh basil leaves

120g baby rocket leaves

80g fetta, crumbled

1 Preheat oven to 220°C/200°C fan-forced.
2 Brush mushrooms with half the oil; place on oven tray. Top each mushroom with 3 tomato halves, cut side up. Bake about 10 minutes or until mushrooms are tender.
3 Meanwhile, place bread slices on oven tray; brush bread with another 2 tablespoons of the oil, rub with garlic. Bake bread slices about 6 minutes or until browned lightly.
4 Blend or process basil with remaining oil until smooth.
5 Top croûtes with rocket, mushrooms and cheese. Drizzle with basil mixture. Sprinkle with extra basil, if desired.
per serving 34.7g fat; 1797kJ (430 cal)

roasted vegetable and haloumi salad

preparation time 15 minutes cooking time 45 minutes serves 4

1 medium kumara (400g), chopped coarsely

2 large carrots (360g), quartered lengthways

2 medium parsnips (500g), halved lengthways

2 cloves garlic, crushed

¼ cup (60ml) extra virgin olive oil

2 large red onions (600g), cut into wedges

4 baby eggplant (240g), halved lengthways

4 fresh long red chillies, halved

250g haloumi, sliced

75g baby spinach leaves

LEMON AND BASIL DRESSING

½ cup (125ml) extra virgin olive oil

2 tablespoons lemon juice

¼ cup coarsely chopped fresh basil leaves

1 teaspoon white sugar

1 Preheat oven to 220°C/200°C fan-forced.

2 Combine kumara, carrots, parsnips and half the combined garlic and oil in large baking dish.

3 Combine onions, eggplant, chilli and remaining oil mixture on oven tray.

4 Roast kumara mixture 15 minutes; place onion mixture in oven; roast both mixtures about 30 minutes or until vegetables are browned and tender.

5 Meanwhile, make lemon and basil dressing.

6 Cook cheese on heated lightly oiled grill plate (or grill or barbecue) until browned lightly.

7 Combine roast vegetables and spinach in large bowl; divide among serving plates. Top with cheese; drizzle with lemon and basil dressing.
   LEMON AND BASIL DRESSING Blend or process ingredients until smooth.
   per serving 53.6g fat; 3035kJ (726 cal)

warm olives with garlic, chilli and oregano

preparation time 5 minutes cooking time 5 minutes serves 8

¾ cup (180ml) extra virgin olive oil

1 fresh long red chilli, sliced thinly

1 clove garlic, sliced thinly

¼ cup coarsely chopped fresh oregano

500g black and green olives

1 Combine oil, chilli, garlic and oregano in heated large frying pan; stir until fragrant.

2 Add olives; shake pan until olives heated through.

3 Serve olives with grissini, if desired.
   per serving 21.2g fat; 1028kJ (246 cal)

falafel

preparation time 15 minutes (plus standing and refrigeration time) cooking time 10 minutes makes 25

¾ cup (135g) dried broad beans

⅔ cup (130g) dried chickpeas

⅓ cup coarsely chopped flat-leaf parsley

2 tablespoons ground cumin

2 tablespoons ground coriander

2 teaspoons salt

1 teaspoon bicarbonate of soda

1 small brown onion (80g), chopped finely

1 tablespoon plain flour

1 egg

vegetable oil, for deep-frying

1 Place beans and chickpeas in separate bowls, cover with water; stand overnight. Drain, rinse separately under cold water; drain.

2 Place beans in medium saucepan of boiling water; return to a boil then simmer, uncovered, 5 minutes. Drain.

3 Blend or process beans, chickpeas, parsley, cumin, coriander, salt, soda, onion, flour and egg until almost smooth. Shape level tablespoons of mixture into patties; place on tray, cover, refrigerate 30 minutes.

4 Heat oil in wok; deep-fry falafel, in batches, until browned. Drain on absorbent paper. Serve falafel with hummus, if desired.
   per falafel 1.2g fat; 96kJ (23cal)

fattoush

preparation time 30 minutes cooking time 5 minutes serves 4

6 pocket pitta

olive oil, for shallow-frying

3 medium tomatoes (450g), chopped coarsely

1 large green capsicum (350g), chopped coarsely

2 lebanese cucumbers (260g), seeded, sliced thinly

10 trimmed red radishes (150g), sliced thinly

4 spring onions (100g), sliced thinly

1½ cups firmly packed fresh flat-leaf parsley leaves

½ cup coarsely chopped fresh mint

LEMON GARLIC DRESSING

2 cloves garlic, crushed

¼ cup (60ml) olive oil

¼ cup (60ml) lemon juice

1 Make lemon garlic dressing.
2 Halve pitta horizontally; cut into 2.5cm pieces. Heat oil in large frying pan; shallow-fry pitta, in batches, until browned lightly and crisp. Drain on absorbent paper.
3 Place about three-quarters of the pitta in large bowl with dressing and remaining ingredients; toss gently to combine. Serve fattoush sprinkled with remaining pitta.
   LEMON GARLIC DRESSING Place ingredients in screw-top jar; shake well.
   per serving 30.6g fat; 2635kJ (630 cal)

bruschetta with eggplant and olive topping

preparation time 15 minutes cooking time 10 minutes serves 4

1 tablespoon olive oil

1 small brown onion (80g), chopped finely

2 cloves garlic, crushed

1 trimmed celery stalk (100g), chopped finely

150g char-grilled eggplant, chopped finely

150g roasted red capsicum, chopped finely

¼ cup (30g) seeded black olives, chopped coarsely

1 tablespoon drained baby capers, rinsed

2 tablespoons roasted pine nuts

¼ cup shredded fresh basil leaves

350g loaf ciabatta

2 tablespoons extra virgin olive oil, extra

1 Heat oil in medium frying pan; cook onion, garlic and celery, stirring, until onion softens. Transfer to medium bowl.

2 Combine eggplant, capsicum, olives, capers, nuts and basil with onion mixture.

3 Cut bread on a slight angle into 8 slices. Brush one side of bread slices with extra oil, grill both sides until toasted.

4 Top toast with eggplant mixture; sprinkle with extra basil leaves, if desired.
   per serving 31g fat; 2274kJ (544 cal)

deep-fried whitebait

preparation time 10 minutes cooking time 15 minutes serves 4

1 cup (150g) plain flour

¼ cup coarsely chopped fresh basil

1 teaspoon garlic salt

500g whitebait

vegetable oil, for deep-frying

SPICED MAYONNAISE DIP

1 cup (300g) mayonnaise

2 cloves garlic, crushed

2 tablespoons lemon juice

1 tablespoon drained capers, rinsed, chopped finely

1 tablespoon coarsely chopped fresh flat-leaf parsley

1 Make spiced mayonnaise dip.
2 Combine flour, basil and garlic salt in large bowl. Toss whitebait in flour mixture, in batches, until coated.
3 Heat oil in wok; deep-fry whitebait, in batches, until browned and cooked through. Drain on absorbent paper. Serve with spiced mayonnaise dip.
   SPICED MAYONNAISE DIP Combine ingredients in small bowl.
   per serving 46.6g fat; 2893kJ (692 cal)

SEAFOOD

tuna, kingfish and salmon carpaccio

preparation time 50 minutes (plus freezing and refrigeration time) serves 6

350g piece sashimi tuna

350g piece sashimi kingfish

350g piece sashimi salmon

⅓ cup (80ml) lime juice

⅔ cup (160ml) lemon juice

4cm piece fresh ginger (20g), grated

¼ cup (60ml) soy sauce

1 baby fennel bulb (130g)

⅓ cup (80ml) extra virgin olive oil

1 tablespoon drained baby capers, rinsed

½ small red onion (50g), sliced thinly

1 teaspoon finely chopped fresh dill

1 Tightly wrap fish, separately, in plastic wrap; freeze about 1 hour or until slightly firm.

2 Unwrap fish then slice as thinly as possible. Arrange slices on separate serving platters; drizzle tuna with lime juice, drizzle kingfish and salmon with lemon juice. Cover platters; refrigerate 1 hour.

3 Meanwhile, combine ginger and sauce in small jug; stand while fish is under refrigeration. Finely chop enough fennel frond tips to make 1 level tablespoon; discard remaining frond tips. Chop fennel bulb finely.

4 To serve, drain excess juice from platters; divide fish among serving plates. Drizzle tuna with strained ginger sauce mixture; sprinkle kingfish with fennel, frond tips and half of the oil; sprinkle salmon with capers, onion, dill and remaining oil. Serve carpaccio with crusty bread, if desired.
per serving 21.1g fat; 1508kJ (361 cal)

lime and coconut prawns

preparation time 15 minutes (plus refrigeration time) cooking time 15 minutes makes 24

24 uncooked medium king prawns (1kg)

⅓ cup (80ml) lime juice

½ cup (125ml) coconut milk

½ cup (75g) plain flour

1½ cups (115g) shredded coconut

peanut oil, for deep-frying

PEANUT DIPPING SAUCE

⅓ cup (45g) roasted unsalted peanuts

⅓ cup (80ml) lime juice

¼ cup (60ml) chicken stock

¼ cup (60ml) coconut milk

2 tablespoons smooth peanut butter

1 tablespoon sweet chilli sauce

1 Shell and devein prawns, leaving tails intact. Combine juice and coconut milk in medium bowl; add prawns, toss to coat in marinade. Cover; refrigerate 1 hour.

2 Meanwhile, make peanut dipping sauce.

3 Drain prawns; reserve marinade. Holding prawns by tail, coat in flour then reserved marinade, then in shredded coconut.

4 Heat oil in wok; deep-fry prawns, in batches, until brown; drain. Serve with warm peanut dipping sauce.
   PEANUT DIPPING SAUCE Combine nuts, juice, stock and coconut milk in small saucepan; bring to a boil. Simmer, uncovered, 5 minutes. Blend or process with peanut butter and sauce until smooth.
   per prawn 8.2g fat; 481kJ (115 cal)

mussels with garlic crumbs

preparation time 20 minutes makes 48

48 medium mussels (1.5kg)

2 cups (500ml) water

100g butter

4 cloves garlic, crushed

¾ cup (50g) stale breadcrumbs

2 teaspoons coarsely chopped fresh chervil

1 Preheat grill.

2 Scrub mussels; remove beards.

3 Place mussels in large saucepan with the water; bring to a boil, simmer, covered, until mussels open (discard any that do not). Discard top shell, loosen mussels from base shell.

4 Melt butter in medium saucepan; stir in garlic and breadcrumbs.

5 Place mussels on oven tray; top with breadcrumb mixture. Grill until browned lightly. Serve sprinkled with chervil.
   per mussel 1.8g fat; 96kJ (23 cal)

chilli salt squid

preparation time 20 minutes cooking time 10 minutes serves 6

Be careful when deep-frying chilli and coriander as the oil may spit and splatter.

1kg squid hoods

vegetable oil, for deep-frying

2 fresh long red chillies, sliced thinly

1 cup loosely packed fresh coriander leaves

⅓ cup (50g) plain flour

2 fresh long red chillies, chopped finely

2 teaspoons sea salt

1 teaspoons ground black pepper

1 Halve squid hoods lengthways, score the insides in crosshatch pattern then cut each half lengthways into five pieces.

2 Heat oil in wok; deep-fry sliced chilli until tender. Drain on absorbent paper. Deep-fry coriander until changed in colour; drain on absorbent paper.

3 Toss squid in combined flour, chopped chilli, salt and pepper. Deep-fry squid, in batches, until tender; drain on absorbent paper. Serve squid sprinkled with coriander and chilli.
per serving 11.8g fat; 1041kJ (249 cal)

bruschetta niçoise

preparation time 35 minutes cooking time 10 minutes makes 48

⅓ cup (80ml) olive oil

3 cloves garlic, crushed

2 small french bread sticks

1 tablespoon drained baby capers, rinsed

1 medium egg tomato (75g), seeded, chopped finely

1 trimmed celery stalk (100g), chopped finely

¼ cup (30g) seeded black olives, chopped finely

180g can tuna in olive oil, drained, flaked

5 drained anchovy fillets, chopped finely

1 small red onion (100g), chopped finely

2 tablespoons lemon juice

1 Combine oil and garlic in small bowl.
2 Preheat grill.
3 Trim ends from bread sticks; cut sticks into 1cm slices. Brush both sides with garlic oil; toast under grill until browned lightly both sides.
4 Combine remaining ingredients in medium bowl. Divide niçoise mixture among bruschetta.
per bruschetta 2.2g fat; 176kJ (42 cal)

chilli garlic octopus

preparation time 10 minutes (plus refrigeration time) cooking time 10 minutes serves 4

1kg cleaned baby octopus, halved

¼ cup (60ml) olive oil

5 cloves garlic, crushed

¼ cup (60ml) lemon juice

2 fresh small red thai chillies, chopped finely

1 Combine ingredients in large bowl; cover, refrigerate 3 hours.
2 Cook octopus, in batches, on heated oiled grill plate (or grill or barbecue) until tender. Serve octopus with lime wedges, if desired.
per serving 18.3g fat; 1831kJ (438 cal)

calamari stuffed with fetta and chilli

preparation time 40 minutes (plus refrigeration time) cooking time 10 minutes serves 8

8 whole calamari with tentacles (600g)

400g firm fetta

1 teaspoon dried chilli flakes

2 tablespoons olive oil

2 tablespoons coarsely chopped fresh oregano

2 teaspoons finely grated lemon rind

2 tablespoons lemon juice

1 clove garlic, crushed

¼ cup (60ml) olive oil, extra

1 To clean the calamari, pull gently on the tentacles to remove. Cut tentacles off below the eyes; discard eyes, the small black beak in the centre of the tentacles and guts. Remove the clear quill from inside the body, then remove the side flaps and dark membrane. Rinse well and pat dry.

2 Mash cheese, chilli, oil and oregano together in small bowl. Spoon cheese mixture into calamari tubes; secure with toothpicks.

3 Place calamari and tentacles in large shallow dish. Pour over combined remaining ingredients; cover, refrigerate 3 hours, turning occasionally.

4 Cook calamari and tentacles on lightly oiled grill plate (or grill or barbecue) about 3 minutes each side or until browned and cheese is heated through.

per serving 24g fat; 1258kJ (301 cal)

vodka-cured gravlax

preparation time 10 minutes (plus refrigeration time) makes 24

1 tablespoon sea salt

1 teaspoon finely ground black pepper

1 tablespoon white sugar

1 tablespoon vodka

300g salmon fillet, skin on

24 mini toasts

SOUR CREAM SAUCE

⅓ cup (80g) sour cream

2 teaspoons drained baby capers, rinsed

2 teaspoons lemon juice

2 teaspoons finely chopped drained cornichons

½ small red onion (50g), chopped finely

1 Combine salt, pepper, sugar and vodka in small bowl.
2 Remove bones from fish; place fish, skin-side down, on piece of plastic wrap. Spread vodka mixture over flesh side of fish; enclose securely in plastic wrap. Refrigerate overnight, turning parcel several times.
3 Make sour cream sauce.
4 Slice fish thinly; spread sauce on toasts, top with fish.
   SOUR CREAM SAUCE Combine ingredients in small bowl.
   per toast 2.4g fat; 230kJ (55 cal)

oysters with tomato capsicum salsa

preparation time 10 minutes makes 24

2 small tomatoes (180g), seeded, chopped finely

1 small red onion (100g), chopped finely

1 small green capsicum (150g), chopped finely

¼ cup (60ml) tomato juice

¼ cup (60ml) lemon juice

1 teaspoon Tabasco sauce

1 tablespoon olive oil

2 cloves garlic, crushed

24 oysters (600g), on the half shell

1 Combine tomatoes, onion, capsicum, juices, sauce, oil and garlic in medium bowl. Serve oysters topped with salsa.
   per oyster 1.1g fat; 96kJ (23 cal)

SEAFOOD

55

smoked seafood and mixed vegetable antipasti

preparation time 35 minutes serves 4

⅓ cup (80g) sour cream

2 teaspoons raspberry vinegar

1 tablespoon coarsely chopped fresh chives

1 clove garlic, crushed

1 large yellow zucchini (150g)

1 tablespoon raspberry vinegar, extra

¼ cup (60ml) extra virgin olive oil

⅓ cup (45g) slivered almonds, roasted

1 cup (150g) drained semi-dried tomatoes

1 large avocado (320g)

1 tablespoon lemon juice

300g hot-smoked ocean trout portions

200g sliced smoked salmon

16 drained caperberries (80g)

1 large lemon (180g), cut into wedges

170g packet roasted garlic bagel crisps

1 Combine sour cream, vinegar, chives and garlic in small bowl, cover; refrigerate until required.

2 Meanwhile, using vegetable peeler, slice zucchini lengthways into ribbons; combine zucchini in small bowl with extra vinegar and 2 tablespoons of the oil.

3 Combine nuts, tomatoes and remaining oil in small bowl.

4 Slice avocado thickly into small bowl; sprinkle with juice.

5 Flake trout into bite-sized pieces.

6 Arrange zucchini mixture, nut mixture, avocado, trout, salmon and caperberries on large platter; serve with sour cream mixture, lemon wedges and bagel crisps.

per serving 54.8g fat; 3624kJ (867 cal)

oysters with pesto butter

preparation time 10 minutes (plus refrigeration time) **cooking time** 5 minutes **makes** 24

125g butter, softened

1 tablespoon lemon juice

2 tablespoons coarsely chopped fresh basil

2 tablespoons roasted pine nuts

24 oysters (600g), on the half shell

1 To make pesto butter, blend or process butter, juice and basil until smooth; fold in nuts. Cover; refrigerate until firm.

2 Preheat oven to 200°C/180°C fan-forced.

3 Divide pesto butter among oysters. Bake about 5 minutes or until butter melts and oysters are heated through.
per oyster 5.5g fat; 242kJ (58 cal)

mini scallop and lime kebabs

preparation time 15 minutes (plus refrigeration time) **cooking time** 5 minutes **makes** 24

2 tablespoons vegetable oil

4cm piece fresh ginger (20g), grated

3 cloves garlic, crushed

24 scallops (600g), roe removed

3 limes

12 fresh kaffir lime leaves, halved lengthways

24 sturdy toothpicks

1 Combine oil, ginger and garlic in medium bowl, add scallops; toss scallops to coat in marinade. Cover; refrigerate 30 minutes.

2 Meanwhile, cut each lime into eight wedges. Skewer one piece of lime leaf and one lime wedge onto each toothpick.

3 Cook scallops on heated oiled grill plate (or grill or barbecue) about 5 minutes or until cooked as desired. Stand 5 minutes then skewer one onto each toothpick.
per kebab 1.8g fat; 134kJ (32 cal)

tip You will need to soak the skewers in water for up to one hour before using to prevent them scorching and splintering during cooking.

salt and pepper prawns

preparation time 20 minutes **cooking time** 5 minutes **serves** 6

18 uncooked large king prawns (1.2kg)

2 teaspoons sea salt

¼ teaspoon five-spice powder

½ teaspoon freshly ground black pepper

1 Shell and devein prawns leaving tails intact. Thread each of the prawns onto a skewer lengthways.
2 Combine remaining ingredients in small bowl.
3 Cook prawn skewers on heated oiled grill plate (or grill or barbecue) over high heat until browned both sides and just cooked through. Sprinkle with half the salt mixture during cooking.
4 Serve prawn skewers with remaining salt mixture.
   per serving 0.5g fat; 309kJ (74 cal)z

scallops with fennel and pernod sauce

preparation time 20 minutes cooking time 30 minutes serves 6

24 scallops, roe removed (600g), on the half shell

60g butter

2 medium fennel bulbs (400g), trimmed, sliced thinly

4 green onions, sliced thinly

⅓ cup (80ml) pernod

300ml cream

1 tablespoon coarsely chopped fennel frond tips

1   Remove scallops from shells; wash shells, dry thoroughly, reserve.
2   Melt two-thirds of the butter in large frying pan; cook fennel, in batches, stirring occasionally, about 20 minutes or until softened.
3   Heat remaining butter in same pan; cook onion, stirring, until soft. Return fennel to pan with scallops, pernod and cream; cook about 2 minutes or until scallops are opaque.
4   Divide shells among serving plates. Using slotted spoon, transfer scallops to shells.
5   Simmer sauce, stirring, until thickens slightly. Spoon sauce over scallops; sprinkle with frond tips.
per serving 30.4g fat; 1588kJ (380 cal)

rösti with smoked salmon

preparation time 30 minutes cooking time 25 minutes makes 24

800g potatoes

15g butter, melted

1 tablespoon finely chopped fresh dill

vegetable oil, for shallow-frying

200g crème fraîche

200g smoked salmon

1 Coarsely grate potatoes; squeeze out as much excess liquid as possible. Combine potatoes, butter and dill in medium bowl.

2 Heat oil in large frying pan. shape level tablespoons of potato mixture into patties; cook patties, in batches, until browned lightly both sides. Drain on absorbent paper.

3 Divide crème fraîche and smoked salmon among rösti. Serve topped with dill sprigs, if desired
per rösti 5.9g fat; 339kJ (81 cal)

antipasti

preparation time 15 minutes cooking time 10 minutes serves 6

400g piece baked ricotta

⅛ teaspoon smoked paprika

¼ teaspoon dried chilli flakes

¼ teaspoon dried oregano leaves

250g cherry tomatoes

½ cup (125ml) extra virgin olive oil

1 medium eggplant (300g), sliced thinly

2 tablespoons small fresh basil leaves

3 chorizo (400g), sliced thinly

¼ cup lightly packed fresh flat-leaf parsley leaves

12 fresh asparagus spears, trimmed

¼ cup (20g) parmesan flakes

10 trimmed red radishes (150g)

150g marinated seeded kalamata olives

1 Preheat oven to 180°C/160°C fan-forced.

2 Place ricotta on shallow oven tray; sprinkle with paprika, chilli and oregano. Place tomatoes on same tray. Drizzle ricotta and tomatoes with 2 tablespoons of the oil; roast about 10 minutes or until tomatoes begin to split.

3 Brush eggplant slices with 2 tablespoons of the oil; cook in grill pan (or pan-fry or barbecue) until browned both sides. Drizzle eggplant with another 1 tablespoon of the oil; top with basil.

4 Cook chorizo in grill pan (or pan-fry or barbecue) until browned both sides; combine in small bowl with parsley.

5 Cook asparagus in large frying pan of simmering water until just tender; drain. Top asparagus with parmesan; drizzle with remaining oil.

6 Serve ricotta, tomatoes, eggplant, chorizo, asparagus, radishes and olives on large platter.
   per serving 34.7g fat; 1797kJ (430 cal)

MEAT & POULTRY

pizza trio

preparation 40 minutes (plus standing time) **cooking time** 10 minutes **makes** 3 thin pizzas
(Each topping quantity given is enough for one pizza. Each pizza makes 5 slices.)

2 teaspoons (7g) dry yeast

½ teaspoon caster sugar

¾ cup (180ml) warm water

2 cups (300g) plain flour

1 teaspoon salt

2 tablespoons olive oil

3 teaspoons olive oil, extra

ANCHOVY OLIVE TOPPING

2 teaspoons olive oil

⅓ cup (80ml) bottled tomato pasta sauce

7 drained anchovy fillets, halved

¼ cup (30g) seeded black olives, halved

12 fresh basil leaves

PANCETTA TOPPING

2 teaspoons olive oil

⅓ cup (80ml) bottled tomato pasta sauce

2 cloves garlic, sliced thinly

½ cup (40g) parmesan flakes

6 thin slices chilli pancetta

SPICY SAUSAGE TOPPING

2 teaspoons olive oil

⅓ cup (80ml) bottled tomato pasta sauce

175g cooked spicy italian sausage

1 fresh long red thai chilli, sliced thinly

100g bocconcini or mozzarella, sliced

2 tablespoons fresh oregano leaves

1 To make pizza dough, combine yeast, sugar and the water in small bowl; cover, stand in warm place about 10 minutes or until frothy. Sift flour and salt into large bowl; stir in yeast mixture and oil; mix to a soft dough. Bring dough together with your hands until ingredients are combined; add a little extra water, if needed.

2 Knead dough on lightly floured surface about 10 minutes or until smooth and elastic, pushing the dough with the heel of your hand and giving it a quarter turn each time. Place dough in lightly oiled large bowl; cover, stand in warm place about 1 hour or until doubled in size.

3 Meanwhile, preheat a covered barbecue.

4 Punch dough down with your fist, then knead on lightly floured surface until smooth. Divide dough into three portions. Roll each portion to about a 16cm x 40 cm rectangle.

5 Layer two pieces of aluminium foil large enough to fit one rectangle of dough. Brush foil with 1 teaspoon of the extra oil; place one portion of dough on top. Repeat process to make two more pizza bases.

6 Turn off burners underneath middle grill plate, leaving outer burners on to cook by indirect heat. Place pizzas, on foil, on grill plate; cover barbecue, cook about 4 minutes or until underneath is browned. (If dough puffs up, flatten quickly with an egg slide.)

7 Carefully remove pizza bases from barbecue, close cover. Turn pizza bases over on foil, brush cooked side with oil, then spread with pasta sauce; top with selected ingredients for each topping except the fresh herbs. Return pizzas to barbecue on foil; cover barbecue, cook 5 minutes or until well browned underneath and crisp. Serve pizzas sprinkled with herbs.
anchovy olive pizza per slice 3.8g fat; 376kJ (90 cal)
pancetta pizza per slice 5.9g fat; 481kJ (115 cal)
spicy sausage pizza per slice 12g fat; 782kJ (187 cal)

Opposite, from top, anchovy olive pizza, pancetta pizza, spicy sausage pizza

lamb and haloumi kebabs

preparation time 20 minutes cooking time 20 minutes makes 8

½ teaspoon ground allspice

1 teaspoon cracked black pepper

1 clove garlic, crushed

2 tablespoons lemon juice

2 tablespoons olive oil

500g diced lamb

200g haloumi, diced into 2cm pieces

1 Place allspice, pepper, garlic, juice and oil in medium bowl; add lamb, turn to coat in mixture. Thread lamb and cheese, alternately, onto skewers.

2 Cook kebabs on heated oiled grill plate (or grill or barbecue) until browned all over and cooked as desired.
   per kebab 28.7g fat ; 1710kJ(409 cal)

sticky-glazed pork with pineapple

preparation time 10 minutes (plus refrigeration time) cooking time 15 minutes makes 32

2 pork fillets (600g)

2 tablespoons char sui sauce

1 tablespoon light soy sauce

½ small pineapple (450g), sliced thinly

½ cup (25g) snow pea sprouts, trimmed

1 Combine pork and sauces in large bowl; refrigerate, covered, 1 hour.

2 Cook pineapple on heated oiled grill plate (or grill or barbecue) until browned lightly. Remove from grill; halve slices, cover to keep warm.

3 Cook pork over low heat on grill plate, covered, about 10 minutes or until cooked. Cover; stand 5 minutes then slice thinly.

4 Top pineapple with 2 slices of pork then sprouts.
   per piece 2.8g fat; 648kJ (155 cal)

veal and tomato dolmades

preparation time 40 minutes cooking time 35 minutes (plus cooling time) makes 36

200g packet grapevine leaves in brine

1 tablespoon olive oil

1 large red onion (300g), chopped finely

4 cloves garlic, crushed

500g veal mince

400g can crushed tomatoes

¼ cup (30g) seeded green olives, chopped finely

¼ cup (35g) drained sun-dried tomatoes, chopped finely

1 tablespoon tomato paste

1 Place leaves in large heatproof bowl, cover with boiling water; stand 10 minutes, drain. Rinse under cold water; drain. Pat 36 similar-sized, well-shaped leaves dry with absorbent paper; reserve remaining leaves for another use.

2 Heat oil in large frying pan; cook onion and garlic, stirring, until onion softens. Add mince; cook, stirring, until just changed in colour.

3 Add remaining ingredients; bring to a boil. Simmer, uncovered, about 5 minutes or until liquid is almost evaporated; cool 15 minutes.

4 Place leaves, vein-side up, on board. Spoon 1 tablespoon of the filling near stem in centre of leaf; roll once toward tip of leaf to cover filling then fold in two sides. Continue rolling toward tip of leaf; place, seam-side down, in baking-paper-lined steamer. Repeat process with remaining leaves and filling mixture, placing rolls about 1cm apart in steamer.

5 Place steamer over large saucepan of boiling water. Steam, covered, about 15 minutes or until dolmades are heated through.

6 Serve hot or cold, drizzled with lemon juice, if desired.
   per dolmade 1.6g fat; 151kJ (36 cal)

roast beef with caramelised onion crostini

preparation time 20 minutes cooking time 30 minutes makes 40

500g beef fillet

1 tablespoon olive oil

2 large red onions (600g), sliced thinly

1 tablespoon brown sugar

1 tablespoon red wine vinegar

1 loaf rye bread (660g)

¼ cup (60ml) olive oil, extra

2 tablespoons mild english mustard

40 fresh flat-leaf parsley leaves

1 Preheat oven to 180°C/160°C fan-forced.

2 Cook beef in heated oiled medium frying pan until browned all over; place in small baking dish. Roast, uncovered, in oven, 20 minutes or until cooked as desired. Wrap beef in foil.

3 Meanwhile, heat oil in pan; cook onion until soft. Add sugar and vinegar; cook, stirring, until caramelised.

4 Discard ends from bread. Cut bread into 1.5cm slices; cut each slice into quarters. Brush bread both sides with extra oil; toast both sides.

5 Slice beef thinly. Spread mustard on bread; top with parsley, beef and onion. Serve at room temperature.

per crostini 3g fat; 339kJ (81 cal)

spicy lamb and pine nut triangles

preparation time 30 minutes cooking time 30 minutes makes 72

10g butter

1 medium brown onion (150g), chopped finely

1 clove garlic, crushed

½ teaspoon ground mixed spice

½ teaspoon freshly ground black pepper

½ cup (80g) roasted pine nuts

2 teaspoons sambal oelek

500g lamb mince

2 green onions, sliced thinly

24 sheets fillo pastry

cooking-oil spray

1 Melt butter in medium frying pan; cook brown onion, garlic, spices, nuts and sambal, stirring, until onion softens. Add lamb; cook, stirring, until lamb is browned and cooked through. Stir in green onion.

2 Preheat oven to 200°C/180°C. Lightly oil two oven trays.

3 Spray one pastry sheet with oil, cover with second pastry sheet; cut crossways into six even strips, spray with oil. Repeat with remaining pastry sheets.

4 Place 2 teaspoons of lamb filling on the bottom of narrow edge of one strip, leaving a 1cm border. Fold corner diagonally across filling to form triangle; continue folding to end of strip, retaining triangle shape. Place triangle on tray, seam-side down; repeat with remaining strips and filling. Spray triangles lightly with oil. Bake about 10 minutes or until browned lightly.

per triangle 1.6g fat; 142kJ (34 cal)

curry puffs with chutney dip

preparation time 40 minutes cooking time 25 minutes makes 32

1 tablespoon vegetable oil

2 green onions, chopped finely

1 clove garlic, crushed

2 teaspoons curry powder

300g beef mince

2 teaspoons lemon juice

⅓ cup (110g) mango chutney

4 sheets ready-rolled puff pastry

1 egg, beaten lightly

⅔ cup (220g) mango chutney, extra

1 tablespoon boiling water

1 Heat oil in medium saucepan; cook onion and garlic, stirring, until onion softens. Add curry powder; cook, stirring, until fragrant. Add beef; cook, stirring, until beef is browned and cooked through. Remove from heat; stir in juice and chutney.

2 Using rolling pin, roll each pastry sheet into 30cm square. Using 8cm-round cutter, cut eight rounds from each pastry sheet.

3 Preheat oven to 200°C/180°C fan-forced. Lightly oil two oven trays.

4 Place one heaped teaspoon of the beef mixture on one round; brush edges with a little egg, fold over to enclose filling. Press edges with fork to seal; repeat with remaining beef mixture and pastry.

5 Place curry puffs on trays; brush with remaining egg. Bake about 15 minutes or until browned lightly.

6 Serve curry puffs with combined extra chutney and the water.
per puff 6.2g fat; 439kJ (105 cal)

beef carpaccio with rocket, parmesan and aïoli

preparation time 20 minutes (plus freezing time) serves 4

400g piece beef fillet, trimmed

80g wild rocket leaves

100g parmesan flakes

AÏOLI

1 egg

1 clove garlic, quartered

1 tablespoon lemon juice

1 tablespoon dijon mustard

½ cup (125ml) olive oil

1   Wrap beef tightly in plastic wrap; place in freezer about 1 hour or until partially frozen.

2   Meanwhile, make aïoli.

3   Using sharp knife, slice unwrapped beef as thinly as possible; divide beef among serving plates.

4   Top beef with rocket and cheese; drizzle with aïoli.
    AÏOLI Blend or process egg, garlic, juice and mustard until combined. With motor operating, add oil in a thin, steady stream until aïoli thickens slightly.
    per serving 44.1g fat; 2211kJ (529 cal)

grilled quail with garlic sauce

preparation time 25 minutes (plus refrigeration time) **cooking time** 30 minutes **serves** 8

12 quail (1.9kg)

1 clove garlic, sliced

2 teaspoons finely grated lemon rind

¼ cup (60ml) olive oil

1 medium red onion (170g), sliced thinly

2 medium tomatoes (300g), seeded, sliced thinly

1 cup firmly packed fresh flat-leaf parsley leaves

2 teaspoons sumac

GARLIC SAUCE

9 cloves garlic, quartered

2 tablespoons lemon juice

1 teaspoon salt

½ cup (125ml) olive oil

1 Cut along both sides of the backbones of quail; remove and discard backbone. Open quail out and place breast-side-up on a board. Press firmly to flatten quail.

2 Combine garlic, rind and oil in shallow dish. Place quails in dish; rub with oil mixture; cover, refrigerate several hours or overnight.

3 Make garlic sauce.

4 Drain quail; reserve marinade. Brush quail with 2 tablespoons of garlic sauce. Cook quail, in batches, on a heated oiled grill plate (or grill or barbecue) about 15 minutes or until cooked.

5 Combine remaining ingredients. Serve quail on salad with garlic sauce.
   GARLIC SAUCE Blend or process garlic, juice and salt until finely chopped. With motor operating, add oil in a thin, steady stream until smooth.
   per serving 33.7g fat; 1685kJ (403 cal)

asparagus and prosciutto frittata

preparation time 25 minutes cooking time 20 minutes makes 48

The frittata can be made a day ahead;
keep, covered, in the refrigerator.

170g thin asparagus

6 eggs, beaten lightly

½ cup (125ml) cream

¼ cup (20g) coarsely grated parmesan

3 slices prosciutto (45g)

½ cup (75g) drained semi-dried tomatoes,
chopped finely

1 Preheat oven to 200°C/180°C fan-forced.

2 Boil, steam or microwave asparagus until just tender; drain. Rinse under
   cold water; drain.

3 Oil 19cm x 29cm slice pan; line base and sides with baking paper.

4 Whisk eggs, cream and cheese in medium bowl until combined.

5 Place asparagus, in single layer, alternating tips and bases, in pan;
   pour over egg mixture. Cook, uncovered, about 20 minutes or until
   firm. Stand 10 minutes in pan.

6 Meanwhile, cut each slice of prosciutto into 16 squares. Cook prosciutto
   in medium frying pan, stirring occasionally, until crisp.

7 Cut frittata into 48 pieces; top each with 1 piece of prosciutto and
   ½ teaspoon of the tomato.
   per piece 2.1g fat; 117kJ (28 cal)

lamb kofta with spiced yogurt

preparation time 30 minutes (plus refrigeration time) **cooking time** 20 minutes **makes** 40

¼ cup (40g) burghul

500g lamb mince

1 egg, beaten lightly

1 medium brown onion (150g), chopped finely

¼ cup (40g) pine nuts, chopped finely

2 tablespoons finely chopped fresh mint

2 tablespoons finely chopped fresh
flat-leaf parsley

vegetable oil, for shallow-frying

SPICED YOGURT

2 fresh small red thai chillies, chopped finely

1 tablespoon finely chopped fresh mint

1 tablespoon finely chopped fresh flat-leaf parsley

1 tablespoon finely chopped fresh coriander

1 clove garlic, crushed

½ teaspoon ground cumin

500g thick yogurt

1　Cover burghul with cold water in small bowl; stand 10 minutes. Drain; pat dry with absorbent paper to remove as much water as possible.

2　Combine burghul in large bowl with lamb, egg, onion, nuts and herbs. Roll rounded teaspoons of the lamb mixture into kofta balls. Place on tray, cover; refrigerate 30 minutes.

3　Heat oil in large frying pan; shallow-fry kofta, in batches, until browned all over and cooked through. Drain on absorbent paper.

4　Meanwhile, combine ingredients for spiced yogurt in medium bowl.

5　Serve kofta hot with spiced yogurt.
per kofta 3.1g fat; 180kJ (43 cal)

spanish tortilla

preparation time 15 minutes cooking time 30 minutes serves 4

800g potatoes, sliced thinly

1 tablespoon olive oil

1 large brown onion (200g), sliced thinly

200g chorizo, sliced thinly

6 eggs, beaten lightly

300ml cream

4 green onions, sliced thickly

¼ cup (25g) coarsely grated mozzarella

¼ cup (30g) coarsely grated cheddar

1   Boil, steam or microwave potato until just tender; drain.

2   Meanwhile, heat oil in medium frying pan; cook brown onion, stirring, until softened. Add chorizo; cook, stirring, until crisp. Drain chorizo mixture on absorbent paper.

3   Whisk eggs in large bowl with cream, green onion and cheeses; stir in potato and chorizo mixture.

4   Pour mixture into heated lightly oiled medium frying pan; cook, covered, over low heat about 10 minutes or until tortilla is just set. Carefully invert tortilla onto plate, then slide back into pan; cook, uncovered, about 5 minutes or until cooked through.

per serving 42.8g fat; 2477kJ (592 cal)

turkish herbed lamb pizza

preparation time 45 minutes (plus standing time) cooking time 35 minutes serves 4

¾ teaspoon dried yeast

1 teaspoon white sugar

¾ cup (180ml) warm water

2 cups (300g) plain flour

1 teaspoon salt

cooking-oil spray

600g lamb mince

1 tablespoon olive oil

1 small brown onion (80g), chopped finely

1 clove garlic, crushed

½ teaspoon ground cinnamon

1½ teaspoons ground allspice

¼ cup (40g) pine nuts, chopped coarsely

¼ cup (70g) tomato paste

2 medium tomatoes (300g), seeded, chopped finely

1 cup (250ml) chicken stock

2 tablespoons lemon juice

¼ cup finely chopped fresh flat-leaf parsley

¼ cup finely chopped fresh mint

½ cup (140g) Greek-style yogurt

2 tablespoons cold water

1 Whisk yeast, sugar and the warm water in small bowl; cover, stand in warm place about 15 minutes or until mixture is frothy.

2 Combine flour and salt in large bowl; stir in yeast mixture, mix to a soft dough. Knead on lightly floured surface about 10 minutes or until smooth and elastic. Place in large oiled bowl, turning dough once to coat in oil. Cover dough; stand in warm place about 1 hour or until dough is doubled in size.

3 Halve dough; knead each portion until smooth then roll out to oval shape measuring approximately 12cm x 35cm. Place each oval on a lightly oiled oven tray; spray lightly with cooking-oil spray. Cover; stand in warm place 30 minutes.

4 Preheat oven to 240°C/220°C fan-forced.

5 Cook mince in heated lightly oiled large frying pan, stirring, until cooked through; place in medium bowl.

6 Heat oil in pan; cook onion and garlic, stirring, until onion softens. Add spices and nuts; cook, stirring, about 5 minutes or until nuts are just roasted. Return mince to pan with tomato paste, tomato, stock and juice; cook, stirring, about 5 minutes or until liquid is almost evaporated. Remove pan from heat; stir in herbs.

7 Spoon mince mixture over pizza bases; cook, uncovered, in oven, about 15 minutes or until bases are cooked through and tops are browned lightly. Serve drizzled with combined yogurt and the cold water.
per serving 26.5g fat; 2805kJ (671 cal)

greek lamb cutlets with skordalia

preparation time 20 minutes (plus refrigeration time) cooking time 10 minutes serves 4

1 tablespoon finely chopped fresh thyme

1 tablespoon finely grated lemon rind

2 teaspoons ground black pepper

1 tablespoon olive oil

1 tablespoon lemon juice

2 cloves garlic, crushed

12 french-trimmed lamb cutlets (480g)

12 sprigs fresh thyme

SKORDALIA

1 slice day-old white bread, crust removed

⅓ cup (80g) mashed potato

1 tablespoon lemon juice

2 cloves garlic, crushed

1 tablespoon olive oil

1 Combine chopped thyme, rind, pepper, oil, juice and garlic in large bowl; add lamb, turn to coat in marinade. Cover; refrigerate 3 hours or overnight.

2 Make skordalia.

3 Cook lamb, in batches, on heated oiled grill plate (or grill or barbecue) until cooked as desired.

4 Serve lamb topped with skordalia and thyme sprigs.

SKORDALIA Cut bread into quarters; soak in small bowl of cold water 2 minutes then squeeze as much water from bread as possible. Blend or process bread, potato, juice and garlic until smooth. With motor operating, add oil; process until smooth.

per serving 20.2g fat; 1095kJ (262 cal)

beef and fig cigars

preparation time 30 minutes cooking time 30 minutes makes 48

Beef mixture can be made the day before and kept, covered, in the refrigerator.

20g butter

1 medium brown onion (150g), chopped finely

½ teaspoon ground cinnamon

2 cloves garlic, crushed

250g beef mince

¾ cup (150g) finely chopped dried figs

1 tablespoon finely chopped fresh chives

8 sheets filo pastry

cooking-oil spray

½ cup (125ml) plum sauce

1 Melt butter in large frying pan; cook onion, cinnamon and garlic, stirring, until onion softens. Add beef; cook, stirring, until beef is browned. Stir in figs and chives; cool 10 minutes.

2 Meanwhile, preheat oven to 200°C/180°C fan-forced. Oil two oven trays.

3 Spray one pastry sheet with oil; cover with a second pastry sheet. Cut lengthways into three even strips, then crossways into four even strips.

4 Place 1 rounded teaspoon of the beef mixture along the bottom of one narrow edge of pastry strip, leaving 1cm border. Fold narrow edge over beef mixture then fold in long sides; roll to enclose filling. Place cigar, seam-side down, on tray; repeat process with remaining pastry and beef mixture.

5 Spray cigars lightly with oil. Bake, uncovered, about 10 minutes or until browned lightly. Serve with plum sauce.
per cigar 0.9g fat; 146kJ (35 cal)

chipotle beef on tortilla crisps

preparation time 15 minutes (plus standing time) cooking time 40 minutes makes 36

2 chipotle chillies

½ cup (125ml) boiling water

12 x 17cm-round white corn tortillas

vegetable oil, for deep-frying

1 tablespoon vegetable oil, extra

1 small brown onion (80g), sliced thinly

1 clove garlic, crushed

300g beef mince

1 tablespoon tomato paste

1 cup (250ml) beer

¼ cup coarsely chopped fresh coriander

½ cup (120g) sour cream

1 Cover chillies with the boiling water in small heatproof bowl; stand 20 minutes.

2 Meanwhile, cut three 7cm-rounds from each tortilla. Heat oil in wok; deep-fry rounds, in batches, until browned lightly. Drain tortilla crisps on absorbent paper.

3 Drain chillies over small bowl; reserve liquid. Remove stems from chillies; discard stems. Blend or process chillies and reserved liquid until smooth.

4 Heat extra oil in medium frying pan; cook onion, stirring, until softened. Add garlic and beef; cook, stirring, until beef is changed in colour. Stir in paste, beer and chilli puree; bring to a boil. Simmer, uncovered, about 15 minutes or until liquid is almost evaporated. Stir in coriander.

5 Top each tortilla crisp with a rounded teaspoon of the chipotle beef then with ½ teaspoon of the sour cream.
   per crisp 3.1g fat; 288kJ (69 cal)

chicken and olive empanadas

preparation time 25 minutes cooking time 40 minutes makes 24

2 cups (500ml) chicken stock

1 bay leaf

3 chicken thigh fillets (600g)

1 tablespoon olive oil

1 small brown onion (80g), chopped finely

2 cloves garlic, crushed

2 teaspoons ground cumin

½ cup (80g) sultanas

⅓ cup (40g) seeded green olives, chopped coarsely

5 sheets ready-rolled shortcrust pastry

1 egg, beaten lightly

1 Place stock and bay leaf in medium frying pan; bring to a boil. Add chicken, reduce heat; poach chicken, covered, about 10 minutes or until cooked through. Cool chicken in liquid 10 minutes; shred chicken finely. Reserve 1 cup of the poaching liquid; discard remainder (or keep for another use).

2 Meanwhile, heat oil in large frying pan; cook onion, stirring, until softened. Add garlic and cumin; cook, stirring, until fragrant. Add sultanas and reserved poaching liquid; bring to a boil. Simmer, uncovered, about 15 minutes or until liquid is almost evaporated. Stir in chicken and olives.

3 Preheat oven to 200°C/180°C fan-forced. Oil two oven trays.

4 Using 9cm cutter, cut 24 rounds from pastry sheets. Place 1 level tablespoon of the filling in centre of each round; fold round in half to enclose filling, pinching edges to seal. Using tines of fork, press around edges of empanadas to make pattern.

5 Place empanadas on trays; brush tops with egg. Bake, uncovered, about 25 minutes or until browned lightly. Serve with yogurt, if desired.
per empanada 11.6g fat; 840kJ (201 cal)

kibbeh

preparation time 40 minutes cooking time 25 minutes makes 25

1½ (240g) burghul

250g lamb mince

½ medium brown onion (75g), chopped finely

3 teaspoons sea salt flakes

olive oil, for deep-frying

FILLING

30g butter

125g lamb mince

½ medium brown onion (75g), chopped finely

2 tablespoons roasted pine nuts

1 fresh long red chilli, chopped finely

1 teaspoon ground allspice

½ teaspoon ground cinnamon

½ teaspoon ground nutmeg

½ teaspoon ground white pepper

pinch saffron threads

1 cinnamon stick

1 bay leaf

1 Soak burghul in warm water 10 minutes; drain.
2 Blend or process burghul, mince, onion and salt until the mixture forms a smooth paste.
3 Make filling.
4 Roll 1½ tablespoons of burghul mixture into balls. Make a small hole in the centre with your finger; fill with one heaped teaspoon of the filling. Roll the ball to enclose filling and form an oval shape. Repeat with remaining burghul mixture and filling.
5 Heat oil in wok; deep-fry balls about 2 minutes or until well-browned. Drain on absorbent paper.
   FILLING Heat butter in small frying pan; cook mince and onion, stirring, until browned lightly. Add nuts, chilli, spices and bay leaf; cook, stirring, 10 minutes. Discard cinnamon stick and bay leaf.
   per kibbeh 4.8g fat; 368kJ (88 cal)

camembert fondue

preparation time 10 minutes cooking time 20 minutes serves 4

Cheese can also be wrapped in foil to bake.

200g camembert

1 tablespoon extra virgin olive oil

1 tablespoon dry white wine

1 clove garlic, crushed

1 teaspoon fresh lemon thyme leaves

1 long french bread stick, sliced thickly

1 Preheat oven to 200°C/180°C fan-forced.
2 Place cheese on large piece of baking paper; drizzle with oil and wine then sprinkle with garlic and thyme. Wrap and seal paper to enclose cheese. Place on oven tray.
3 Bake about 20 minutes or until centre of the cheese is soft.
4 Open paper, serve cheese with sliced bread to dip.
   per serving 20.6g fat; 1743kJ (414 cal)

CHEESE

cheese balls with four coatings

preparation time 40 minutes (plus refrigeration time) **makes** 64

500g neufchâtel cheese

500g farm cheese

2 teaspoons finely grated lemon rind

2 tablespoons lemon juice

¼ teaspoon sea salt

PEPPER COATING

1½ tablespoons poppy seeds

2 teaspoons cracked black pepper

PARSLEY COATING

¼ cup finely chopped fresh flat-leaf parsley

SESAME SEED COATING

¼ cup (35g) sesame seeds

ZA'ATAR COATING

1 tablespoon sumac

1 tablespoon toasted sesame seeds

1 teaspoon dried oregano

1 teaspoon dried marjoram

1 teaspoon sweet paprika

2 teaspoons dried thyme

1 Line four oven trays with baking paper.
2 Blend or process ingredients until smooth; refrigerate about 2 hours or until firm enough to roll.
3 Roll rounded teaspoons of the mixture into balls; place 16 balls on each tray. Refrigerate, covered, until firm.
4 Combine ingredients for pepper coating in small bowl. Combine ingredients for za'atar coating in separate small bowl.
5 Roll 16 balls in each of the four coatings. Serve cold.
   pepper coating per ball 4.5g fat; 217kJ (52 cal)
   parsley coating per ball 4.4g fat; 210kJ (50 cal)
   sesame seed coating per ball 4.7g fat; 224kJ (53 cal)
   za'atar coating per ball 4.5g fat; 217kJ (52 cal)

Opposite, from left, pepper coating, parsley coating, sesame seed coating, za'atar coating

goat cheese croûtes with herbs

preparation time 15 minutes cooking time 5 minutes serves 6

½ long french bread stick

¼ cup (60ml) extra virgin olive oil

2 cloves garlic, crushed

150g soft goat cheese

1 tablespoon finely chopped fresh chives

1 tablespoon coarsely chopped fresh chervil

1 tablespoon extra virgin olive oil, extra

1 teaspoon sea salt flakes

1 Preheat grill.
2 Slice bread diagonally into 1cm-thick slices. Place slices on oven tray; brush with combined oil and garlic. Place under grill until browned lightly both sides.
3 Spoon cheese into serving bowl; top with herbs, drizzle with extra oil then sprinkle with salt. Serve cheese with croûtes.
   per serving 10.4g fat; 598kJ (143 cal)

deep-fried mozzarella sticks

preparation time 10 minutes cooking time 10 minutes makes 32

1 cup (150g) plain flour

1 cup (150g) cornflour

2 eggs, beaten lightly

1½ cups (375ml) water

1 cup (100g) packaged breadcrumbs

500g mozzarella

vegetable oil, for deep-frying

CHILLI PESTO DIPPING SAUCE

⅓ cup (90g) sun-dried tomato pesto

⅔ cup (160ml) sweet chilli sauce

1 Make chilli pesto dipping sauce.
2 Whisk flour, cornflour, egg and the water in medium bowl until smooth. Place breadcrumbs in small bowl.
3 Cut cheese into 1cm-wide sticks.
4 Dip cheese sticks, one at a time, in batter, then in breadcrumbs to coat. Double coat cheese sticks by dipping, one at a time, back in batter, then in breadcrumbs.
5 Heat oil in wok; deep-fry cheese sticks, in batches, until golden brown. Drain on absorbent paper.
6 Serve hot with chilli pesto dipping sauce.
   CHILLI PESTO DIPPING SAUCE Combine ingredients in small bowl.
   per stick 6.1g fat; 479kJ (114 cal)

marinated cherry bocconcini with prosciutto

preparation time 20 minutes (plus standing time) **makes** 40

2 cloves garlic, crushed

1 long green chilli, chopped finely

⅓ cup (80ml) olive oil

40 cherry bocconcini (600g)

10 slices thin prosciutto (150g)

1 bunch fresh basil

1 Combine garlic, chilli and oil in medium bowl. Add cheese; toss to coat in mixture. Stand 30 minutes.
2 Halve prosciutto slices crossways, then half again lengthways.
3 Drain cheese; reserve marinade. Wrap one piece of prosciutto and one basil leaf around each cheese piece; secure with a toothpick.
4 Serve drizzled with reserved marinade.
   per piece 3.7g fat; 188kJ (45 cal)

grilled haloumi

preparation time 5 minutes cooking time 5 minutes serves 8

Haloumi is a salty, stretched-curd cheese available at delicatessens and most supermarkets.

1 tablespoon olive oil

400g haloumi, sliced thinly

2 tablespoons drained pickled green chillies

1 medium lemon (140g), cut into wedges

125g large black olives

125g large green olives

1   Heat oil in large frying pan; cook cheese, in batches, until browned lightly.
2   Arrange cheese on serving platter with chillies, lemon and olives. Serve with pitta, if desired.
    per serving 11.2g fat; 736kJ (176 cal)

grilled fetta

preparation time 5 minutes cooking time 5 minutes serves 6

300g fetta, halved

2 tablespoons olive oil

1 teaspoon dried chilli flakes

1 teaspoon dried oregano leaves

1   Preheat grill.
2   Place cheese on large sheet of foil; place on oven tray. Combine oil, chilli and oregano in small bowl; press over cheese. Grill about 5 minutes or until browned lightly. Stand 5 minutes; slice thickly.
    per serving 17.8g fat; 817kJ (195 cal)

mozzarella and sun-dried tomato risotto balls

preparation time 5 minutes **cooking time** 50 minutes (plus cooling time) **makes** 30

2 cups (500ml) chicken stock

½ cup (125ml) water

1 tablespoon olive oil

1 small brown onion (80g), chopped finely

1 clove garlic, crushed

¾ cup (150g) arborio rice

1 tablespoon finely chopped fresh basil

1 tablespoon finely chopped fresh flat-leaf parsley

2 tablespoons finely chopped semi-dried tomatoes

60g mozzarella, diced into 1cm pieces

¼ cup (25g) packaged breadcrumbs

vegetable oil, for deep-frying

1 Place stock and the water in medium saucepan; bring to a boil. Simmer, covered.

2 Meanwhile, heat olive oil in medium saucepan; cook onion and garlic, stirring, until onion softens. Add rice; stir to coat in onion mixture. Stir in ½ cup of the simmering stock mixture; cook, stirring, over low heat until liquid is absorbed. Continue adding stock mixture, in ½-cup batches, stirring, until liquid is absorbed after each addition. Total cooking time should be about 35 minutes or until rice is just tender. Stir in herbs and tomato, cover; cool 30 minutes.

3 Roll heaped teaspoons of the risotto mixture into balls; press a piece of cheese into centre of each ball, roll to enclose. Coat risotto balls in breadcrumbs.

4 Heat vegetable oil in wok; deep-fry risotto balls, in batches, until browned lightly and heated through.
per ball 2.5g fat; 201kJ (48 cal)

bocconcini, olive and cherry tomato skewers with pesto

preparation time 25 minutes makes 32

You need 32 long cocktail toothpicks for this recipe.

½ cup (40g) finely grated parmesan

½ cup (80g) roasted pine nuts

2 cloves garlic, crushed

1 cup (250ml) extra virgin olive oil

2 cups firmly packed fresh basil leaves

16 cherry tomatoes, halved

32 cherry bocconcini (480g)

32 medium seeded green olives (110g)

1 Blend or process cheese, nuts, garlic and half the oil until combined. Add basil and remaining oil; process until almost smooth. Transfer pesto to serving bowl.

2 Thread one tomato half, one bocconcini and one olive onto each toothpick.

3 Serve skewers with pesto.

per skewer 2.2g fat; 142kJ (34 cal)

goat cheese and asparagus tarts

preparation time 20 minutes cooking time 20 minutes makes 24

3 sheets ready-rolled shortcrust pastry

10g butter

150g asparagus, chopped finely

2 cloves garlic, crushed

1 tablespoon chopped fresh thyme leaves

150g soft goat cheese

2 eggs, beaten lightly

⅔ cup (160ml) cream

1 Preheat oven to 200°C/180°C fan-forced. Grease two 12-hole (2 tablespoons/40ml) patty pans.

2 Using 7cm cutter, cut 24 rounds from pastry; place rounds into patty pan holes.

3 Heat butter in small frying pan; cook asparagus, garlic and half the thyme, stirring, about 5 minutes or until asparagus is just tender. Divide asparagus mixture and cheese among pastry cases.

4 Combine egg and cream in small jug; pour over asparagus and cheese mixture. Sprinkle with remaining thyme leaves.

5 Bake, uncovered, about 15 minutes or until browned lightly.

per tart 10.4g fat; 598kJ (143 cal)

CHEESE

ALLSPICE also known as pimento or jamaican pepper; available whole or ground. Tastes like a blend of cinnamon, clove and nutmeg.

ALMONDS flat, pointy-tipped nuts having a pitted brown shell enclosing a creamy white kernel that is covered by a brown skin.
slivered small pieces cut lengthways.

ARTICHOKE GLOBE large flower-bud of a member of the thistle family; it has tough leaves and is edible in part when cooked.

BEANS

broad also known as fava, windsor and horse beans; available dried, fresh, canned and frozen. Fresh should be peeled twice (discarding both the outer long green pod and the beige-green tough inner shell); the frozen beans have had their pods removed but the beige shell still needs removal.

butter also known as lima beans; large, flat, kidney-shaped bean, off-white in colour, with a mealy texture and mild taste. Available both canned and dried.

BICARBONATE OF SODA also known as baking soda; used as a leavening agent.

BREAD

mini toasts small bread slices that have been toasted. Available from most supermarkets and delicatessens.

ciabatta means slipper in Italian, which is the traditional shape of this popular crisp-crusted, open-textured white sourdough bread.

BREADCRUMBS

packaged fine-textured, crunchy, purchased, white breadcrumbs.

stale 1- or 2-day-old bread made into crumbs by grating, blending or processing.

BUTTER use salted or unsalted ("sweet") butter; 125g is equal to 1 stick butter.

BURGHUL also known as bulghur wheat; hulled steamed wheat kernels that, once dried, are crushed into various size grains. Is not the same as cracked wheat.

CAPERBERRIES olive-sized fruit formed after the buds of the caper bush have flowered; usually sold pickled in a vinegar brine.

CAPERS grey-green buds of a warm climate (usually mediterranean) shrub, sold either dried and salted or pickled in a vinegar brine.

CAPSICUM also known as bell pepper or, simply, pepper. Can be red, green, yellow, orange or purplish black. Discard seeds and membranes before use.

CARDAMOM can be purchased in pod, seed or ground form. Has a distinctive aromatic, sweetly rich flavour, and is one of the world's most expensive spices.

CAYENNE PEPPER *see chilli.*

CHEESE

blue mould-treated cheeses mottled with blue veining. Varieties include firm and crumbly stilton types to mild, creamy brie-like cheeses.

bocconcini baby mozzarella; from the diminutive of boccone meaning mouthful. A walnut-sized, delicate, semi-soft white cheese traditionally made from buffalo milk. Spoils rapidly so must be kept under refrigeration, in brine, for 1 or 2 days at most.

cheddar the most widely eaten cheese in the world; a semi-hard cow-milk cheese. It ranges in colour from white to pale yellow, and the flavour becomes sharper with time.

fetta a crumbly textured goat- or sheep-milk cheese having a sharp, salty taste. Ripened and stored in salted whey.

fontina a smooth firm cheese with a nutty taste and a brown or red rind.

goat made from goats' milk; has an earthy, strong taste. Available in soft, crumbly and firm textures, in various shapes and sizes, and sometimes rolled in ash or herbs.

haloumi a firm, creamed-coloured sheep-milk cheese matured in brine; tastes like a minty, salty fetta in flavour. Haloumi can be grilled or fried, briefly, without breaking down.

mozzarella soft, spun-curd cheese; originating in southern Italy where it was traditionally made from water-buffalo milk, now, generally, manufactured from cow milk. It is the most popular pizza cheese because of its low-melting point and elasticity when heated (used for texture rather than flavour).

parmesan also known as parmigiano; is a hard, grainy cow-milk cheese that originated in the parma region of Italy. Can be grated or flaked and used for pasta, salads and soups. Reggiano is the best parmesan, aged for a minimum 2 years and made only in the Italian region of Emilia-Romagna.

ricotta a soft, sweet, moist, white, cow-milk cheese with a low fat content (about 8.5 per cent) and a slightly grainy texture. The name roughly translates as "cooked again" and refers to ricotta's manufacture from a whey that is itself a by-product of other cheese making.

CHERVIL also known as cicily; mildly fennel-flavoured herb with curly dark-green leaves.

CHICKPEAS also called garbanzos, hummus or channa; an irregularly round, sandy-coloured legume used extensively in Mediterranean, Indian and Hispanic cooking. Has a firm texture, even after cooking, a floury mouth-feel and robust nutty flavour; available canned or dried (the latter need several hours reconstituting in cold water before being used).

CHILLIES available in many different types and sizes, both fresh and dried. Generally the smaller the chilli, the hotter it is; use rubber gloves when seeding and chopping fresh chillies as they can burn your skin.

cayenne pepper a thin-fleshed, long, extremely hot red chilli; purchased dried and ground.

chipotle hot, dried, smoked jalapeños, available in cans.

dried flakes deep-red, dehydrated chilli slices and whole seeds; use in cooking or as a condiment for sprinkling over cooked foods.

red thai small, medium hot and bright red.

sweet chilli sauce *see sauces.*

CHORIZO SAUSAGE a sausage of Spanish origin, made of coarsely ground pork and highly seasoned with garlic and chillies.

COCONUT

cream is obtained commercially from the first pressing of the coconut flesh alone, without the addition of water.

milk not the juice found inside the fruit, which is known as coconut water, but the diluted liquid from the second pressing (less rich) of the grated mature coconut flesh.

CORIANDER also known as cilantro or chinese parsley when fresh; bright-green-leafed herb with a pungent flavour. Both the stems and roots of coriander are also used in Thai cooking; wash well before chopping. Coriander seeds and ground coriander must never be used to replace fresh coriander or vice versa. The tastes are completely different.

GLOSSARY

CORNICHON French for gherkin, a very small variety of pickled cucumber.

CREME FRAICHE a mature, naturally fermented cream (minimum fat content 35 per cent) having a velvety texture and slightly tangy, nutty flavour. Crème fraîche, a french variation of sour cream, can boil without curdling and can be used in both sweet and savoury dishes.

CUCUMBER, LEBANESE short, slender and thin-skinned. Probably the most popular variety because of its tender, edible skin, tiny, yielding seeds and sweet, fresh and flavoursome taste.

CUMIN also known as zeera or comino; is the dried seed of a plant related to parsley family having a spicy, nutty flavour. Available in seed form or dried and ground.

EGGPLANT purple-skinned vegetable also known as aubergine. can be purchased char-grilled in jars.
baby eggplant also known as finger or japanese eggplant; very small and slender so can be used without disgorging.

FENNEL also known as finocchio or anise; a crunchy green vegetable slightly resembling celery that's eaten raw in salads, fried as an accompaniment, or used as an ingredient in pasta sauces, soups and sauce. Also the name given to the dried seeds of the plant, which have a stronger licorice flavour.

FIVE-SPICE POWDER a fragrant mixture of ground cinnamon, clove, star anise, sichuan pepper and fennel seeds. Also known as chinese five-spice.

FLOUR
besan also known as chickpea flour or gram; made from ground chickpeas so is gluten-free and high in protein. Used in Indian cooking to make chapati.
plain an all-purpose flour, made from wheat.
self-raising plain flour sifted with baking powder in the proportion of 1 cup flour to 2 teaspoons baking powder.

GINGER also known as green or root ginger; the thick gnarled root of a tropical plant. Can be kept, peeled, covered with dry sherry, in a jar and refrigerated, or frozen in an airtight container. *Ground ginger*, also known as powdered ginger, is used as a flavouring in cakes, pies and puddings and cannot be substituted for fresh ginger.
pickled pink or red coloured; available, packaged, from Asian food shops. Pickled paper-thin shavings of ginger in a mixture of vinegar, sugar and natural colouring; mostly used in Japanese cooking.

GRAPEVINE LEAVES from early spring, fresh grapevine leaves can be found in most specialist greengrocers. Alternatively, cryovac-packages containing leaves in brine can be found in Middle Eastern food shops and some delicatessens; rinse and dry well before using.

HUMMUS a Middle-Eastern salad or dip made from softened dried chickpeas, garlic, lemon juice and tahini (sesame seed paste); can be purchased, ready-made, from delicatessens and supermarkets.

KIPFLER POTATO small, finger-shaped, nutty flavour; great baked and in salads.

KUMARA Polynesian name of orange-fleshed sweet potato often confused with yam.

MINCE MEAT also known as ground meat, as in beef, veal, lamb, pork and chicken.

MUSHROOMS
button small, cultivated white mushrooms having a delicate, subtle flavour. When a recipe in this book calls for an unspecified type of mushroom, use button.
flat large, flat mushrooms with a rich, earthy flavour, ideal for filling and barbecuing. They are sometimes misnamed field mushrooms, which are wild mushrooms.
shiitake when fresh are known as chinese black, forest or golden oak mushrooms; although cultivated, they have the earthiness and taste of wild mushrooms. Are large and meaty; often used as a substitute for meat in some Asian vegetarian dishes. When dried, they are known as donko or dried chinese mushrooms; rehydrate before use.
swiss brown also known as cremini or roman mushrooms; are light brown mushrooms having a full-bodied flavour. Button or cup mushrooms can be substituted.

MUSTARD
dijon also known as french. Pale brown, creamy, fairly mild french mustard.
english the traditional hot, pungent, deep yellow mustard. Serve with roast beef and ham; wonderful with hard cheeses.
wholegrain also known as seeded; a coarse-grain mustard made from crushed mustard seeds and dijon-style mustard.

OIL
cooking spray we use a cholesterol-free cooking spray made from canola oil.
olive made from ripened olives. *Extra virgin* and *virgin* are the first and second press of the olives and are, therefore, considered the best; the *extra light* or *light* name on other types refers to taste not fat levels.
vegetable any of a number of oils sourced from plants rather than animal fats.

OLIVES
kalamata small, sharp-tasting, brine-cured black olives.
niçoise small black olives.

ONIONS
baby also known as cocktail or pickling onions. Belonging to a group classified as "dry" onions, these small brown onions are pickled raw in brine.
brown and white these can be used interchangeably. Their pungent flesh adds flavour to a vast range of dishes.
green also known as scallion or, incorrectly, shallot; an immature onion picked before the bulb has formed, having a long, bright-green edible stalk.
red also known as spanish, red spanish or bermuda onion; a sweet-flavoured, large, purple-red onion.
shallots also called french shallots, golden shallots or eschalots. small, elongated, brown-skinned members of the onion family; they grow in tight clusters similar to garlic.
spring have a crisp, narrow green-leafed top and a round sweet white bulb that is larger than the green onion.

PANCETTA an Italian unsmoked bacon; pork belly is cured in salt and spices then rolled into a sausage shape and dried for several weeks. Used sliced or chopped as an ingredient rather than eaten on its own; can also be used to add taste and moisture to tough or dry cuts of meat.
hot pancetta is lean pork belly first salted and cured then spiced and rolled into a fat loaf; used in pasta sauces and meat dishes.

PARSLEY, FLAT-LEAF also known as continental parsley or italian parsley.

PAPRIKA ground dried sweet red capsicum (bell pepper); there are many grades and types available, including sweet, hot, mild and smoked.

PASTRY
fillo also known as phyllo; tissue-thin pastry sheets purchased chilled or frozen that are easy to work with and very versatile, lending themselves to both sweet and savoury dishes.
puff, ready-rolled packaged sheets of frozen puff pastry.
shortcrust, ready-rolled packaged sheets of frozen shortcrust pastry; is easier and quicker to make than richer pastries. Traditionally the pastry is made by rubbing fat into the flour with the finger tips until the mixture resembles breadcrumbs.

PERNOD is a licorice-flavoured liqueur that is often drunk diluted with ice and water, which turns it a cloudy white.

PIDE also known as turkish bread. Comes in long (about 45cm) flat loaves as well as individual rounds; made from wheat flour and sprinkled with sesame or black onion seeds.

PINE NUTS also known as pignoli; not really nuts, but small, cream-coloured kernels from the cones of several types of pine tree.

PITTA also known as lebanese bread; wheat-flour pocket bread sold in large, flat pieces that separate into two thin rounds. Also available in small thick pieces known as pocket pitta.

POLENTA a flour-like cereal made of ground corn (maize); similar to cornmeal but coarser and darker in colour. Also the name of the dish made from it.

PROSCIUTTO a kind of unsmoked Italian ham; salted, air-cured and aged, it is usually eaten uncooked.

QUAIL small, delicate-flavoured game birds ranging in weight from 250g to 300g; also known as partridge.

RICE

arborio small, round-grain rice well-suited to absorb a large amount of liquid; especially suitable for risottos.

basmati a white, fragrant long-grained rice; the grains fluff up beautifully when cooked. Wash several times before cooking.

jasmine or thai jasmine, is a long-grained white rice recognised around the world as having a perfumed aromatic quality; moist in texture, it clings together after cooking. Sometimes substituted for basmati rice.

SAMBAL OELEK (also spelled ulek or olek) Indonesian in origin; a salty paste made from ground chillies and vinegar.

SAUCES

char siu a chinese barbecue sauce made from sugar, water, salt, fermented soybean paste, honey, soy sauce, malt syrup and spices. it can be found at most supermarkets.

soy made from fermented soy beans. Light soy sauce is light in colour but generally quite salty, while salt-reduced soy sauce contains less salt. Several variations are available in most supermarkets and Asian food stores.

sweet chilli comparatively mild, Thai-type sauce made from red chillies, sugar, garlic and white wine vinegar.

Tabasco brand name of an extremely fiery sauce made from vinegar, hot red chillies and salt.

worcestershire a thin, dark-brown spicy sauce used as a seasoning and condiment.

SEAFOOD

calamari a type of squid; substitute with baby octopus.

mussels should be bought from a fish market where there is reliably fresh fish; they must be tightly closed when bought, indicating they are alive. Before cooking, scrub the shells with a strong brush and remove the beards; discard any shells that do not open after cooking. Varieties include black and green-lip.

octopus are usually tenderised before you buy them; both octopus and squid require either long slow cooking (large molluscs) or quick cooking over high heat (small molluscs), anything in between will make the octopus tough and rubbery.

oysters available in many varieties, including pacific, bay, blacklip and New Zealand or Sydney rock oysters.

prawns also known as shrimp. Varieties include, school, king, royal red, Sydney and tiger. Can be bought uncooked (green) or cooked, with or without shells.

sashimi raw fish pieces that have all the skin and bones removed.

scallops a bivalve mollusc with a fluted shell valve; we use scallops that have the coral (roe) attached unless indicated.

squid also known as calamari; a type of mollusc. Buy squid hoods to make preparation and cooking faster.

whiting (sand whiting) also known as silver whiting, summer whiting, King George whiting or trumpeter. Substitute with bream.

SPRING ROLL WRAPPERS sometimes called egg roll wrappers; they come in various sizes and can be purchased fresh or frozen from Asian supermarkets.

SUGAR

brown extremely soft, fine granulated sugar retaining molasses for its characteristic colour and flavour.

caster also known as superfine or finely granulated table sugar.

palm also known as jaggery, gula jawa and gula melaka; made from the sap of the sugar palm tree. Dark brown to black in colour and usually sold in rock-hard cakes. Available from Asian food stores; dark brown sugar can be substituted, if necessary.

white granulated table sugar; also known as crystal sugar.

SUMAC a purple-red, astringent spice ground from berries growing on shrubs that flourish wild around the Mediterranean. It adds a tart, lemony flavour. Available from Middle-Eastern food stores.

TAHINI sesame seed paste available from Middle Eastern food stores; most often used in Lebanese recipes such as hummus.

TOFU also known as bean curd; an off-white, custard-like product made from the "milk" of crushed soy beans. Comes fresh as soft or firm, and processed as fried or pressed dried sheets. Leftover fresh tofu can be refrigerated in water (which is changed daily) for up to 4 days. *Silken tofu* is not a type of tofu but reference to the manufacturing process of straining soybean liquid through silk; this denotes best quality.

TURMERIC also known as kamin. Is a rhizome related to galangal and ginger; must be grated or pounded to release its somewhat acrid aroma and pungent flavour.

VINEGAR

balsamic made from a regional wine of white Trebbiano grapes specially processed then aged in antique wooden casks to give the exquisite pungent flavour. Originally from Modena, Italy, there are now many balsamic vinegars on the market ranging in pungency and quality depending on how long they have been aged.

raspberry made from fresh raspberries steeped in a white-wine vinegar.

white wine made from white wine.

VODKA an un-aged clear spirit distilled from grains such as barley, wheat or rye; also available in various citrus flavours.

WASABI an asian horseradish used to make the pungent green-coloured sauce traditionally served with Japanese raw fish dishes; sold in powdered or paste form.

WHOLE EGG MAYONNAISE commercial mayonnaise of high quality made with whole eggs and labelled as such; some prepared mayonnaises substitute emulsifiers such as food starch, cellulose gel or other thickeners to achieve the same thick and creamy consistency. Must be refrigerated once opened.

WITLOF also known as chicory or belgian endive. Cigar-shaped tightly packed heads with pale, yellow-green tips. Has a delicately bitter flavour.

YEAST a raising agent used in dough making. Granular (7g sachets) and fresh compressed (20g blocks) yeast can almost always be substituted one for the other.

ZUCCHINI also known as courgette; small, pale- or dark-green, yellow or white vegetable belonging to the squash family. Harvested when young, its edible flowers can be stuffed then deep-fried or oven-baked.

MEASURES

One Australian metric measuring cup holds approximately 250ml; one Australian metric tablespoon holds 20ml; one Australian metric teaspoon holds 5ml.

The difference between one country's measuring cups and another's is within a two- or three-teaspoon variance, and will not affect your cooking results. North America, New Zealand and the United Kingdom use a 15ml tablespoon.

All cup and spoon measurements are level. The most accurate way of measuring dry ingredients is to weigh them. When measuring liquids, use a clear glass or plastic jug with the metric markings.

We use large eggs with an average weight of 60g.

DRY MEASURES

METRIC	IMPERIAL
15g	½oz
30g	1oz
60g	2oz
90g	3oz
125g	4oz (¼lb)
155g	5oz
185g	6oz
220g	7oz
250g	8oz (½lb)
280g	9oz
315g	10oz
345g	11oz
375g	12oz (¾lb)
410g	13oz
440g	14oz
470g	15oz
500g	16oz (1lb)
750g	24oz (1½lb)
1kg	32oz (2lb)

LIQUID MEASURES

METRIC	IMPERIAL
30ml	1 fluid oz
60ml	2 fluid oz
100ml	3 fluid oz
125ml	4 fluid oz
150ml	5 fluid oz (¼ pint/1 gill)
190ml	6 fluid oz
250ml	8 fluid oz
300ml	10 fluid oz (½ pint)
500ml	16 fluid oz
600ml	20 fluid oz (1 pint)
1000ml (1 litre)	1¾ pints

LENGTH MEASURES

METRIC	IMPERIAL
3mm	⅛in
6mm	¼in
1cm	½in
2cm	¾in
2.5cm	1in
5cm	2in
6cm	2½in
8cm	3in
10cm	4in
13cm	5in
15cm	6in
18cm	7in
20cm	8in
23cm	9in
25cm	10in
28cm	11in
30cm	12in (1ft)

OVEN TEMPERATURES

These oven temperatures are only a guide for conventional ovens.
For fan-forced ovens, check the manufacturer's manual.

	°C (CELSIUS)	°F (FAHRENHEIT)	GAS MARK
Very slow	120	250	½
Slow	150	275-300	1-2
Moderately slow	160	325	3
Moderate	180	350-375	4-5
Moderately hot	200	400	6
Hot	220	425-450	7-8
Very hot	240	475	9

CONVERSION CHART

ARE YOU MISSING SOME OF THE WORLD'S FAVOURITE COOKBOOKS?

The Australian Women's Weekly Cookbooks are available from bookshops, cookshops, supermarkets and other stores all over the world. You can also buy direct from the publisher, using the order form below.

TITLE	RRP	QTY	TITLE	RRP	QTY
Asian, Meals in Minutes	£6.99		Japanese Cooking Class	£6.99	
Babies & Toddlers Good Food	£6.99		Kids' Birthday Cakes	£6.99	
Barbecue Meals In Minutes	£6.99		Kids Cooking	£6.99	
Beginners Cooking Class	£6.99		Lean Food	£6.99	
Beginners Simple Meals	£6.99		Low-carb, Low-fat	£6.99	
Beginners Thai	£6.99		Low-fat Feasts	£6.99	
Best Food	£6.99		Low-fat Food For Life	£6.99	
Best Food Desserts	£6.99		Low-fat Meals in Minutes	£6.99	
Best Food Fast	£6.99		Main Course Salads	£6.99	
Best Food Mains	£6.99		Mexican	£6.99	
Cakes Biscuits & Slices	£6.99		Middle Eastern Cooking Class	£6.99	
Cakes Cooking Class	£6.99		Midweek Meals in Minutes	£6.99	
Caribbean Cooking	£6.99		Muffins, Scones & Breads	£6.99	
Casseroles	£6.99		New Casseroles	£6.99	
Chicken	£6.99		New Classics	£6.99	
Chicken Meals in Minutes	£6.99		New Finger Food	£6.99	
Chinese Cooking Class	£6.99		New Salads (Oct 06)	£6.99	
Christmas Cooking	£6.99		Party Food and Drink	£6.99	
Chocolate	£6.99		Pasta Meals in Minutes	£6.99	
Cocktails	£6.99		Potatoes	£6.99	
Cooking for Friends	£6.99		Salads: Simple, Fast & Fresh	£6.99	
Detox	£6.99		Saucery	£6.99	
Dinner Beef	£6.99		Sauces Salsas & Dressings	£6.99	
Dinner Lamb	£6.99		Sensational Stir-Fries	£6.99	
Dinner Seafood	£6.99		Short-order Cook	£6.99	
Easy Australian Style	£6.99		Slim	£6.99	
Easy Curry	£6.99		Stir-fry	£6.99	
Easy Spanish-Style	£6.99		Superfoods for Exam Success	£6.99	
Essential Soup	£6.99		Sweet Old Fashioned Favourites	£6.99	
French Food, New	£6.99		Tapas Mezze Antipasto & other bites	£6.99	
Fresh Food for Babies & Toddlers	£6.99		Thai Cooking Class	£6.99	
Get Real, Make a Meal	£6.99		Traditional Italian	£6.99	
Good Food Fast	£6.99		Vegetarian Meals in Minutes	£6.99	
Great Lamb Cookbook	£6.99		Vegie Food	£6.99	
Greek Cooking Class	£6.99		Weekend Cook	£6.99	
Grills	£6.99		Wicked Sweet Indulgences	£6.99	
Healthy Heart Cookbook	£6.99		Wok, Meals in Minutes	£6.99	
Indian Cooking Class	£6.99		TOTAL COST:	£	

Mr/Mrs/Ms _____

Address _____

_____ Postcode _____

Day time phone _____ Email* (optional) _____

I enclose my cheque/money order for £ _____

or please charge £ _____

to my: ☐ Access ☐ Mastercard ☐ Visa ☐ Diners Club

PLEASE NOTE: WE DO NOT ACCEPT SWITCH OR ELECTRON CARDS

Card number ☐☐☐☐ ☐☐☐☐ ☐☐☐☐ ☐☐☐☐ ☐☐☐☐

Expiry date _____ 3 digit security code *(found on reverse of card)* _____

Cardholder's name_____ Signature _____

To order: Mail or fax – photocopy or complete the order form above, and send your credit card details or cheque payable to: Australian Consolidated Press (UK), Moulton Park Business Centre, Red House Road, Moulton Park, Northampton NN3 6AQ, phone (+44) (0) 1604 497531 fax (+44) (0) 1604 497533, e-mail books@acpmedia.co.uk or order online at www.acpuk.com
Non-UK residents: We accept the credit cards listed on the coupon, or cheques, drafts or International Money Orders payable in sterling and drawn on a UK bank. Credit card charges are at the exchange rate current at the time of payment.
Postage and packing UK: Add £1.00 per order plus 50p per book.
Postage and packing overseas: Add £2.00 per order plus £1.00 per book.
All pricing current at time of going to press and subject to change/availability.
Offer ends 31.12.2007

* By including your email address, you consent to receipt of any email regarding this magazine, and other emails which inform you of ACP's other publications, products, services and events, and to promote third party goods and services you may be interested in.